Country Summers with Nanna

Written by: Quisetter White

Illustrated by: Amy Rottinger

Enjoy! ☺

Quisetter White

xoxo

Halo
PUBLISHING
INTERNATIONAL

ISBN: 978-1-61244-915-9
LCCN: 2020919323

Halo Publishing International, LLC
8000 W Interstate 10, Suite 600
San Antonio, Texas 78230
www.halopublishing.com

Printed and bound in the United States of America

This book is dedicated to Ethel Frederick aka "Nanna." Thank you for the best summers of my life and for instilling in me the belief that I can do anything. I'll always keep pushing no matter what.

Love Always & Forever,

Quisetter aka "Shug"

It's the last day of school and I'm so excited! Summer break means traveling to the country and my heart is delighted.

I'm headed to North Carolina to hang out with my Nanna. It's the best part of the year— even more important than Santa.

I help my family pack up the car with luggage and lots of treats. We play games, read books and listen to songs on repeat.

I yell out, "I Spy" and describe the things that I see. But my mom and my uncles can't seem to guess correctly to beat me.

We arrive at the house and Nanna hurries to greet us. She tells us, "Took ya'll long enough!" and hugs us all during her rant and friendly fuss.

The warmth of her embrace makes me feel safe. And her smile tells me I am always welcome in her humble yet cozy home.

I love the smell of Nanna's soft curly hair—
coconut oil and notes of shea butter linger
in the air. Her beautiful thick eyebrows and
smooth, sun-kissed skin helped me believe
being Black was beautiful and not a sin.

Her laugh is radiant, hearty and infectious
as can be. Whenever something is funny
she smacks her knee, chuckles and says,
"Ahhh Me!"

We spend much of our time talking and cooking in the kitchen. She shows me how to snap peas and mix cornbread and shares exciting stories while I listen.

She always fixes food with love as our laughter radiates from the kitchen. My uncles and cousins try to sneak food while we aren't paying attention.

Delicious dinners mix with conversations down memory lane, reminiscing about how my momma inherited her funny nickname.

At night we sit on the porch and talk about my hopes and dreams, while I try to catch fireflies in my hands to watch them gleam.

Nanna always tells me I can do anything my heart desires. She says I need to have faith, believe in myself and work hard even when I am tired.

Nanna prays for me, gives me advice and makes me smile. I pray for her too and make her laugh with my witty style.

She calls me her "Shug," a special nickname
just for me. And she'll always be my Nanna-
the woman that holds my heart and fills
my summers with such glee.